THE POCKET LIBRARY OF GREAT ART

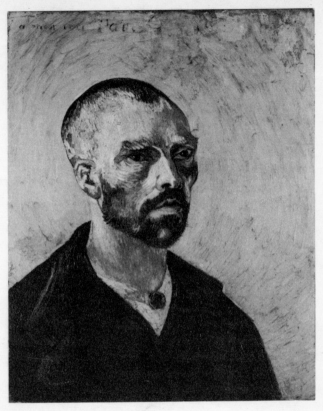

Plate 1. SELF-PORTRAIT. *1888. Oil*
Fogg Art Museum, Cambridge (Wertheim Collection)

VINCENT

VAN GOGH

(1853–1890)

text by

ROBERT GOLDWATER

Associate Professor of Art, Queens College, New York

published by HARRY N. ABRAMS, INC., *in association with* POCKET BOOKS, INC., *New York*

On the cover

OLD PEASANT *(see color plate 16)*

Plate 2. GARDEN OF NUENEN VICARAGE. *1884. Ink and pencil*
Collection V. W. van Gogh, Laren

Vincent

In July, 1880, just ten years before his life ended,
Vincent van Gogh wrote to his brother Theo of his
decision to become a painter. He was twenty-seven,
had unsuccessfully tried to be picture dealer, school-
master, bookseller, and evangelist, and had suffered
much anguished doubt that he was good for anything
at all. To his puritan family, who believed in the
close connection of work and morality, he seemed
an idler and a non-conforming eccentric. Actually he

was a man with a calling, but still uncertain of what that calling was.

Vincent van Gogh the painter did not break with his own past. The dramatic single events of Van Gogh's career, in which he seems at the mercy of outside forces or uncontrollable factors within himself, must never obscure for us the strength of the steadfast determination by which he set his course. The zeal, the conviction remained the same. He was not a success as a picture dealer because he tried to alter the taste of his clients through argument; as an evangelist he had been too wholehearted and fundamental a samaritan, carrying his gospel into immediate practice. He was a dedicated and partisan artist. He had admired compassion in literature (Shakespeare, Dickens, Hugo, and Harriet Beecher Stowe) and in art (Rembrandt, Israels, Daumier, and Millet). He was a compassionate painter. The love he had thrice offered to women and which had been rejected he poured out in his pictures. He had been aghast at the misery of the London slums and the mining fields of Belgium. He was himself "eternally" poor and found in working people one of his great subjects of inspiration. He reached his decision to be an artist slowly and painfully, and now he was determined to work through the "invisible iron wall that seems to stand between what one *feels* and what one *can do,*" to "undermine that wall and file through it slowly and patiently" in the knowledge that "great things are not something accidental but must certainly be willed."

Van Gogh, then, was a painter for only a decade. His mature work was produced in even fewer years,

Plate 3. THE POTATO EATERS. *1885. Ink. Courtesy J. K. Thannhauser, New York*

Plate 4. STUDIES OF HANDS. *1885. Crayon. Collection V. W. van Gogh, L*

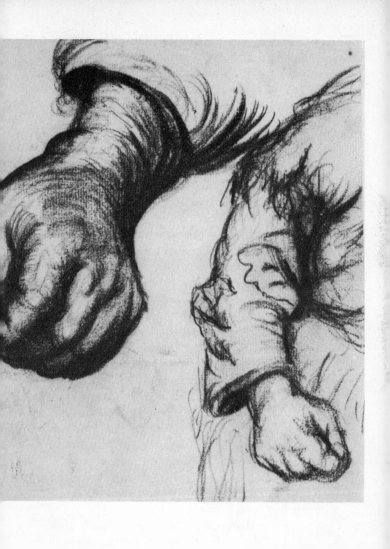

for preparation was needed. First Brussels, visiting the museum, studying anatomy and perspective; then several months at home, ending in an unhappy love affair and misunderstandings with his father; then followed nearly two years at The Hague, three months in the desolate north country region in Holland, and another year with his family; then three months in Antwerp, and in February, 1886, the decisive impulse to join his brother Theo in Paris.

His subjects during this time were still life, landscape, and his beloved peasants. He painted a series of portrait heads, another of weavers at their looms, and *The Potato Eaters*. His palette was dark, based on his native Rembrandt tradition and on Millet and Corot, and he endowed his figures with a coarse but sympathetic dignity.

In Paris the great revelation was the Impressionists, with their rainbow colors and their broad, broken brush strokes. He had been prepared for this by a study of Delacroix and his Antwerp enthusiasm for Rubens. But now his palette is transformed and becomes clear and light. In Paris he discovers the Japanese print, which inspires him to a new boldness of design. He comes to know Toulouse-Lautrec, Pissarro, Degas, Seurat, Signac, and Gauguin. His canvases hang alongside theirs in the smaller dealers' shops. Like them he paints the Seine, the boulevards, the heights of Montmartre, the flag-decked streets on Bastille Day. But his work has a force and directness of attack that is all his own.

And then in February, 1888, just two years after his arrival in Paris, Van Gogh left for the south of France. There, in the town of Arles, he entered upon

Plate 5. OLD MAN IN GRIEF. *1882. Pencil*
Collection V. W. van Gogh, Laren

the final, most productive period of his life. He was greeted by snow, but soon came the southern spring and the southern sun, revealing to this northerner a sudden glory of color and bursting forth of vernal growth that prompted him to a tremendous artistic fecundity. As always he was without money, living entirely on the generosity of his brother Theo; yet he was full of optimism. He found quarters and friends among the citizens of Arles, and invited Gauguin down to begin his cooperative "atelier of the future." He painted without letup in his room, in the fields in the hot sun, at night in the cafés, turning out pictures with rapidity, clarity of vision, and assurance.

His letters to his brother were now resumed, and in them we can follow almost day by day the details of Vincent's life: the nagging worry about money, never having enough, always trying to spend less; the constant, but constantly disappointed, hope that his pictures will sell; nevertheless, his faith in the work he and his brother are doing *together*—because only Theo's support makes his painting possible; he discusses his insight into the essential character of his themes and his desire for expression through color. This correspondence with his brother, together with the letters to his fellow-artists (Van Rappard, Emile Bernard, Gauguin), is one of the great documents of artistic creation, a testimony to Van Gogh's fixity of purpose.

The first of Van Gogh's attacks of illness (sometimes diagnosed as epilepsy but still uncertain) occurred on the day before Christmas, 1888, while Gauguin was with him in Arles. He was well again very quickly, but in May, 1889, yielding to pressure

Plate 6. THE STATE LOTTERY. 1882. Crayon. Collection V. W. van Gogh, Laren

from his neighbors, he asked to go to the asylum in nearby Saint-Rémy. He lived there for a year, and in May, 1890, moved to Auvers, to be near Theo and Theo's wife and son. He continued to paint at a feverish pace, but became increasingly melancholy, and in July, 1890, he shot himself. Van Gogh's suicide was no unpremeditated impulse. He had been conscious of possible insanity for over ten years; for a year and a half there had been increasing interruptions in his work. Faced with the prospect of soon not being able to work at all, he could no longer in conscience be a burden to his brother. To Theo he left his pictures, their joint creation.

Van Gogh's painting is an art of high intensity, created under pressure by a man of extreme sensitivity, conveying his insight, his immediate feeling, and his intense conviction. But it is also the work of a painter, created with awareness by an artist of extraordinary sensibility, and embodying his knowledge, his considered judgment and his aesthetic understanding. His art has meaning entirely through his pictorial method. He said, "It was 'only pictures full of painting' that I did." He also said, "I believe in the absolute necessity for a new art of color, of design, and— of artistic life." He created such an art, and in so doing pointed the way to others—inspired by his life and by his work.

Plate 7. PEASANT WOMAN. *1885. Crayon*
Collection V. W. van Gogh, Laren

Plate 8. A PEASANT DIGGING. *About 1885. Crayon*
Collection V. W. van Gogh, Laren

COLOR PLATES

PLATE 9

Painted November, 1884–April, 1885, Nuenen

STILL LIFE: HAT AND PIPE

Kröller-Müller State Museum, Otterlo

14¾ x 21"

All his life Van Gogh was concerned with everyday objects and everyday people. In this still life, painted before he adopted the light, bright colors of the Impressionists, he is exploring the relation of solid objects in space, setting down the rhythm of spatial intervals in depth. He does this in the traditional fashion, with a source of illumination from the side, and a dark background to set off the volumes of bottle, pot, hat, and jar—each a variation on the circle, and all contrasted with the underlying rectangular structure of the table. Van Gogh deliberately rejected conventional technical facility and preferred to achieve such grave rhythms through simple means.

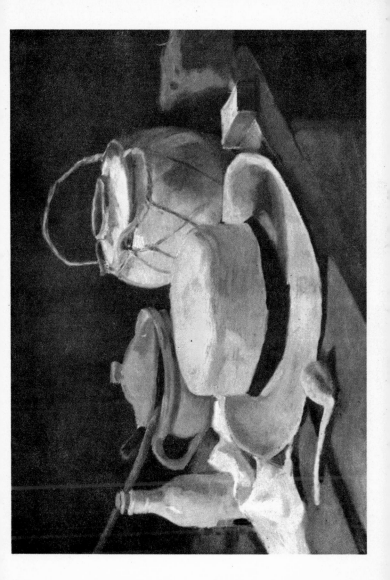

PLATE 10

Painted August, 1888, Arles

SUNFLOWERS

Tate Gallery, London

$37\frac{3}{8} \times 28\frac{3}{4}''$

Here—after the impact of Impressionism, Paris, and the south—the problem has changed. (See plate 9.) Instead of light on dark, there is light on light; instead of a diagonal table in depth, a single band across the bottom of the canvas; instead of a raking source of light producing shading and cast shadows, a suffusion of brilliant color and no traditional modeling at all; instead of warm and cold colors in alternation, a picture predominantly yellow heightened only by touches of green. It is a silhouette without perspective, yet it is full of space. This is a picture glowing with life, painted in a spirit of objective study.

PLATE 11

Painted December, 1888–January, 1889, Arles

VAN GOGH'S CHAIR

Tate Gallery, London

$35\frac{1}{2}$ x 28"

What gives this picture its expressive power? Is it Van Gogh's conscious concern with the effect of light? Perhaps in part, for he has changed a chair of unpainted wood into yellow in order to heighten its contrast with the red and to achieve an integrated harmony of color. But beyond the problems of design is the utter seriousness with which the painter regarded such familiar objects, a respect so profound as almost to transform them into living beings. Like the rest of his bedroom in Arles (plate 20) they become symbols of stability in Van Gogh's world of continual crisis.

Plate 12. THE ORCHARD *(commentary follows color plate section)*

PLATE 13

Painted 1887, Paris

PERE TANGUY

Collection Mr. and Mrs. Edward G. Robinson
Beverly Hills, California

25 x 19"

Père Tanguy was a simple man who sold artists' sup-
plies in Paris. His customers became his friends, and
on occasions when they lacked money he was willing
to exchange brushes and colors for pictures. Père
Tanguy's shop became a kind of informal gallery
where many of the Post-Impressionist group hung
their canvases. In this portrait he is framed by some
of the Japanese prints which Van Gogh during this
period came to know and to admire for their brilliant
color and sure design. In the composition of this picture their energy makes a curious contrast to the
hieratic stiffness of the figure.

PLATE 14

Painted August, 1888, Arles

THE POSTMAN ROULIN

Museum of Fine Arts, Boston

$31\frac{1}{4} \times 25''$

Of this postman, who became his good friend, Van Gogh said he was "a man more interesting than most," and he likened him to Père Tanguy. Van Gogh was interested in painting the "blue uniform trimmed with gold," but also in rendering his character, for he remarked on the "big bearded face, very like Socrates." He has captured the awkward sincerity of the man, who is not used to posing, and the stiffness of the whole body suddenly conscious of its spread-out weight. Above all, in the utterly candid expression, and the wonderfully gnarled hands, which even in repose cannot lose the animation of their long labors, he has given us an unsentimental portrait of one of the simple people with whom he felt most at ease. Yet Van Gogh could write: "I do not know if I can paint the postman *as I feel him.*"

PLATE 15

Painted May, 1888, Arles

THE DRAWBRIDGE

Wallraf-Richartz Museum, Cologne

20¼ x 26⅜"

Van Gogh painted such small, sparsely balanced draw-bridges many times. In this version, there are many reminders of how much Van Gogh took from Oriental art, especially the Japanese print: the angular lines of the scene, viewed from the side; the contrast of the slender upright of the evergreens with the flat expanse of the bridge and its approaches; and the smallness of the figures sympathetically lost against the sky. The silhouette of the delicate structure of the bridge itself suggests the East. Yet one suspects that Vincent was attracted to this theme for another, more personal and nostalgic reason: this bridge must also have reminded him of the small bridges over the canals of his native Holland.

LIFT FOLD FOR ENTIRE PAINTING →

DETAIL AT RIGHT

Painted August, 1888, Arles

OLD PEASANT (PATIENCE ESCALIER)

Collection Mrs. Chester Beatty, London

$27\frac{3}{4}$ x $22\frac{3}{4}$"

"Instead of trying to reproduce exactly what I have before my eyes, I use color more arbitrarily so as to express myself more forcibly," Van Gogh wrote. "I think of the man I have to paint, terrible in the furnace of the full harvest, the full south. Hence the strong orange shades, vivid as a red-hot iron, and hence the luminous tones of old gold in the shadows."

Like *The Postman* (plate 14) this picture is evidence of how quickly and how far Van Gogh had traveled from Impressionism. The colors he had learned to use in Paris are now reinforced by the brilliant sun of the south. But the brush stroke is more vigorous and varied: as an example, it follows the contour of the forms around the eyes; it is limited by outline where strength requires, as over the right shoulder; and it is contrasted where necessary with flat, brilliant areas.

AT RIGHT: DETAIL OF COVER PLATE

PLATE 17

Painted August–November, 1888, Arles

PORTRAIT OF ARMAND ROULIN

Folkwang Museum, Essen

$25\frac{5}{8} \times 21\frac{1}{4}''$

This painting of the sixteen-year-old son of the post-man Roulin is one of a series. Van Gogh conceived these portraits as a group and, through them, saw himself achieving intimate contact with a social unit and creating in the portraits a psychological document. He said that this project partially consoled him for not being a doctor, emphasizing once more his strong desire to come close to people and to nature through his art. The easy manner of this picture, its broad, thin areas of paint and cool colors, contrasts with the incisive lines and hot tones of the *Old Peasant;* here it is expressive of hopeful youth.

Plate 18. THE NIGHT CAFE *(commentary follows color plate section)*

PLATE 19

Painted September, 1889, Saint-Rémy

PORTRAIT OF THE ARTIST

Collection Mr. and Mrs. John Hay Whitney, New York
$22\frac{3}{8} \times 17\frac{1}{8}''$

Like his countryman, Rembrandt, whose human qualities he so much admired, and like his contemporary, Cézanne, Van Gogh often painted himself. Cézanne "used himself as a model" quite simply and usually objectively; Rembrandt, observing himself with an Olympian detachment, recorded his changing features as though he were Everyman. Van Gogh always paints his own personal self, observant, sensitive, and receptive, yet also immediately responsive and wary of the intensity of his own emotion in the face of a world to which he could not help but react with feeling. He holds his palette in a tight grasp, and the concentration of the pose suggests that he is braced against the shock of what he sees. Yet his eyes are unwavering in their gaze, while the brilliant silhouette and flame-like hair are bravely set off against a somber background.

PLATE 20

Painted October, 1888, Arles

VAN GOGH'S BEDROOM

The Art Institute of Chicago

28½ x 36"

Van Gogh conceived this picture—painted, as he said, with "the shadows suppressed . . . in free flat washes like the Japanese prints"—as a contrast to the *Night Café*. "This time it's just simply my bedroom, only here color is to do everything . . . is to be suggestive here of *rest* or sleep in general. In a word, to look at the picture ought to rest the brain or rather the imagination."

What strikes us besides, in contrast to the *Night Café,* is the friendliness of this scene, filled with square, solid objects among which Van Gogh was literally at home. The instability of the outside world is gone, and one can imagine the worrying tension of the brows of the *Portrait of the Artist* relaxing in the atmospnere of this refuge.

LIFT FOLD FOR ENTIRE PAINTING →

DETAIL AT RIGHT

Painted July, 1888, Arles

"L A   M O U S M E"

National Gallery of Art, Washington, D. C.
(Chester Dale Collection, Loan)

28¾ x 23¾"

Like all great portraitists, but perhaps more intuitively than most, Van Gogh adapted his approach to suit the personality of the sitter. In this portrait of a young girl, the colors are light, the areas of blouse and skirt are broken by contrasting hues, giving at once a feeling of intensity and lightness. The back and arms of the chair repeat in fuller amplitude the graceful curves of the figure itself. The light green background, which serves as a foil to the colors of the dress, is subtly repeated in the cuffs and the sprig of oleander. Contrast Van Gogh's handling of this portrait with the bolder forms of the two that follow.

PLATE 25

Painted May, 1890, Saint-Rémy

ROAD WITH CYPRESSES

Kröller-Müller State Museum, Otterlo

35¾ x 28"

Van Gogh described this picture, one of the last he did in the south, in a letter to Gauguin: "A cypress with a star, a last attempt—a night sky with a moon without radiance, the slender crescent barely emerging from the opaque shadow cast by the earth—a star with exaggerated brilliance. Very romantic if you like, but Provence also I think." Here, in all its virtuosity and controlled effect, is the wonderful brush stroke of these later pictures, tying together pictorial surface and perspective depth, as it unites the flow of the road with the movement of the heavens. The "late way-farers" are small, but still at home in the spectacle around them, and the single cypress holds its own against the universal panorama.

ENTIRE PAINTING AT RIGHT

LIFT FOLD FOR DETAIL ⟶

Painted November, 1888, Arles

L'ARLESIENNE (MADAME GINOUX)

The Metropolitan Museum of Art, New York
(Bequest of Samuel A. Lewisohn)

$35\frac{3}{8}$ x $28\frac{3}{8}$"

This canvas was painted while Gauguin was staying with Vincent in Arles, in their abortive attempt to realize Van Gogh's ideal of a cooperative colony of artists. It is surprising in several ways. Van Gogh rarely paints in such flat surfaces or such definite outlines and rarely creates such clear and simple patterns. It is surely Gauguin's own style which influences him in this direction. At the same time, the rhythmic outline of sleeve and hair and coif, the pyramidal structure of the whole figure, inverted and repeated in elbow, jabot, and chin, give this painting an impressive three-dimensional monumentality. One would never suspect from its air of dignity and calm that it was set down on canvas, complete, within an hour!

PLATE 2 3

Painted June, 1890, Auvers

PEASANT GIRL

Collection A. Hahnloser, Winterthur, Switzerland

36¼ x 28¾"

In contrast to the two previous portraits, the active surface here is the background. To set the figure off, Van Gogh has used the unbroken areas of the big yellow hat and apron, and the rich blue of the bodice. The background of wheat brings the whole figure forward, and in its activity suggests the strength that is embodied in the firmly-cut features and in the hands, even in repose. Here is a mature strength very different from the young grace of *La Mousmé,* or the dowager-like immobility of *L'Arlésienne.*

PLATE 24

Painted June, 1889, Saint-Rémy

THE STARRY NIGHT

Museum of Modern Art, New York
(Lillie P. Bliss Collection)

28¾ x 36¼"

Our first impression is the rolling rhythm of the sky—as much like the sea as the heavens—that seems to fill the whole canvas. But presently we see that this is no cataclysm engulfing the earth. The tree shoots up in flame-like projection, and the village nestles tranquilly around its church beneath a surge of sky that is not so much awful as magnificent.

For an explanation of the kind of symbolism Van Gogh aimed at we can do no better than to quote the artist himself, writing to his brother a year earlier from Arles: "I am always in hope of making a discovery (in the study of color), to express the love of two lovers by a marriage of two complementary colors, their mingling and their opposition, the mysterious vibrations of kindred tones. . . . To express hope by some star, the eagerness of a soul by a sunset radiance. Certainly there is nothing in that of stereoscopic realism, but is it not something that actually exists?"

LIFT FOLD FOR ENTIRE PAINTING →

DETAIL AT RIGHT

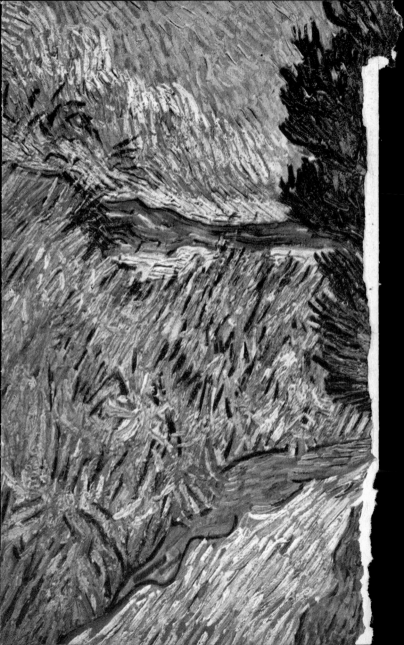

Painted June, 1888, Arles

FISHING BOATS ON THE BEACH AT SAINTES-MARIES

Collection V. W. van Gogh, Laren

25⅜ x 31⅞"

Van Gogh spent a week at Saintes-Maries, a village on the Mediterranean twenty-five miles south of Arles, which gets its name from the three Marys who according to legend landed there in 45 A.D. "On the beach," he wrote, "there are little boats, green, red, and blue, so pretty in form and color that one is reminded of flowers." And he painted their crossed gaffs like a spiky plant whose lines are repeated in the anchor on the sand and the gull in the sky. It was venturesome to paint their flat colors side by side and to put the dark tones in the midst of an otherwise predominantly light harmony of melting and nuanced colors.

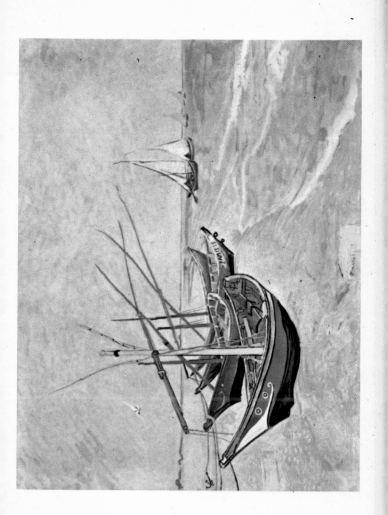

Plate 27. OLIVE ORCHARD *(commentary follows color plate section)*

Painted September, 1888, Arles

SIDEWALK CAFE AT NIGHT

Kröller-Müller State Museum, Otterlo

31 x 24¾"

The deep perspective, the combination of brilliant
yellow under the gas light and the intense blue of the
night sky, the lighted windows in the dark buildings,
the small figures defined by a few elliptical lines—these
are things Van Gogh learned how to handle from his
study of the Japanese print. The very use of the night
scene, with its dramatic contrasts of tone and hue and
its concentration of human society against the vastness
of the distant sky, suggests how far Van Gogh has come
from the pleasant, fused, and sunlit world of the
Impressionists.

Painted March, 1888, Arles

THE ORCHARD

Collection V. W. van Gogh, Laren. 23⅝ x 31⅞"

In its clarity, gaiety, and comparative objectivity, this springtime scene is still an Impressionist painting. It employs the sunlit Impressionist palette, which Van Gogh saw in Paris in 1886, and is among the first recordings of the brilliant effects of the southern sun, which he encountered in Arles just before this picture was painted. At first glance this is a happy and tranquil picture. Yet if we look closely we see that this is after all Van Gogh. The trees are outlined and their shapes are brittle and staccato in rhythm. The field from which they grow is built of strong, vertical strokes whose intensity contrasts with the softness of the flowering orchard above.

Painted September, 1888, Arles

THE NIGHT CAFE

Collection Stephen C. Clark, New York. 27½ x 35"

"I have tried to express the terrible passions of humanity by means of red and green." Into this commonplace scene Van Gogh has put something of the drama he carried within himself. The room contains only the standard inventory of a French provincial café. The excitement stems from the exaggerated perspective, the expansion of the empty central space, the shrunken size of the few figures (each group separate and withdrawn into itself); from the symbolic radiation of the oil lamps, and the deliberate, unrealistic contrast of yellow, red, and green. He wrote, "I have tried, as it were, to express the powers of darkness in a low drink-shop, by soft Louis XV green and malachite, contrasting with yellow green and hard blue greens, and all this in an atmosphere like a devil's furnace, of pale sulphur. And all this under an appearance of Japanese gaiety, and the good nature of Tartarin."

COMMENTARY FOR COLOR PLATE 27

Painted September-October, 1889, Saint-Rémy

OLIVE ORCHARD

Kröller-Müller State Museum, Otterlo. 28 x 35⅜"

In the changing moods of Van Gogh's canvases it is sometimes the inner, sometimes the outer, sources of emotion that dominate. *The Starry Night* is a projection of the painter's feelings, a thoroughly Expressionist conception. In this *Olive Orchard*, on the other hand, the unity originates in the naturalistic grasp of the tree shapes, brought together by a pervasive emphasis on their characteristic twisted forms. As the shapes are like each other, so the colors are close-knit, and the repetition of the bent trunks is matched by the even recession of the trees into the background. "What I have done," wrote Van Gogh to his brother, "is rather hard and coarse reality . . . but it will give a sense of the country and will smell of the soil."

Plate 29. PEASANT OF THE CAMARGUE. *1888. Ink*
Collection Thorsten Laurin, Stockholm

Plate 30. OLD MAN IN THE ALMSHOUSE. *1882. Pencil*
Collection V. W. van Gogh, Laren

Plate 31. BEHIND THE SCHENKWEG, THE HAGUE. *1882. Crayon. Kröller-Müller State Museum, Otterlo*

Plate 32. PEASANTS DIGGING. About 1885. Chalk. Kröller-Müller State Museum, Otterlo

Plate 33. BOATS ANCHORED. *1888. Pen. Coll. Edith Wetmore, New York*

Plate 34. THE STARRY NIGHT. *1889-90. Ink. Museum, Bremen*

Plate 35. FOUNTAIN IN THE HOSPITAL GARDEN. *1889-90. Ink*
Collection V. W. van Gogh, Laren

Plate 36. PEASANTS AT DINNER. *1889-90. Crayon. Collection V. W. van Gogh, Laren*

Plate 37. COTTAGE AND CYPRESSES. *1889-90. Crayon*
Collection V. W. van Gogh, Laren

Plate 38. AVENUE OF POPLARS. *About 1885. Ink*
Collection V. W. van Gogh, Laren

BIOGRAPHICAL NOTES

1853   Vincent van Gogh (English pronunciation, *van-GOH*) born March 30, Groot-Zundert, Holland. Brother Theo born in 1857.

1869–76   Works for the art dealers Goupil in The Hague, London, and Paris.

1877–79   Works as bookseller. Studies unsuccessfully for the ministry in Amsterdam and Brussels. Is evangelist in the Belgian mining fields; dismissed for his uncompromising zeal.

1880   Resolves to become a painter. Supported by Theo, studies art in Brussels.

1881–85   Studies and paints in The Hague and Nuenen and in Antwerp where he is near starvation.

1886–87   Lives with Theo in Paris. Meets Pissarro, Seurat, Toulouse-Lautrec, Gauguin, Bernard. Influenced by Impressionists, Japanese prints.

1888   Moves to Arles where with Gauguin he hopes to found an artists' colony. Mentally distraught, he attacks Gauguin, cuts off his own ear.

1889   Moves to asylum at Saint-Rémy near Arles; enjoys long periods of sanity between attacks.

1890   Increasing despondency despite laudatory article in *Mercure de France* and sale of landscape in Brussels. Moves to Auvers where he shoots himself and dies on July 29. Theo dies six months later.

Drenthe, Holland, 1883. "The world only concerns me insofar as I feel a certain debt and duty towards it because I have walked on that earth for thirty years, and, out of gratitude want to leave some souvenir in the shape of drawings or pictures—not made to please a certain tendency in art, but to express a sincere human feeling."

Nuenen, Holland, 1885. "I should be desperate if my figures were correct. . . . I adore the figures by Michelangelo though the legs are undoubtedly too long, the hips and the backsides too large. . . . My great longing is to learn to make those very incorrections, those deviations, remodelings, changes of reality, that they may become, yes, untruth if you like—but more true than the literal truth."

Arles, France, 1888. "You know, whatever this sacrosanct Impressionism may be, all the same I wish I could paint things that the generation *before* — Delacroix, Millet, Rousseau, Diaz, Monticelli . . . a heap of others could understand. Ah, Manet has been very, very near it, and Courbet. The marrying of form and color."

Arles, 1888. "And in a picture I want to say something comforting as music is comforting. I want to paint men and women with that something of the eternal which the halo used to symbolize, and which we seek to give by the actual radiance and vibration of our coloring."

From *The Letters of Vincent van Gogh to his Brother, 1872-1886* and *Further Letters of Vincent van Gogh to his Brother, 1886-1890,* reprinted by permission of Constable & Co., London.

SOME OTHER BOOKS
ABOUT VAN GOGH

The Letters of Vincent van Gogh to his Brother, 1872-1886. Boston, Houghton Mifflin, 1927

Further Letters of Vincent van Gogh to his Brother, 1886-1890. Boston, Houghton Mifflin, 1929

Dear Theo, The Autobiography of Vincent van Gogh, ed. Irving Stone. Boston, Houghton Mifflin, 1937 (Selections from Van Gogh's letters arranged as a continuous autobiography)

J. B. de la Faille. *L'Oeuvre de Vincent van Gogh.* Paris and Brussels, Van Oest, 1928 (Complete catalogue of the graphic work)

J. B. de la Faille. *Vincent van Gogh.* Paris, Hyperion, 1939. (Complete catalogue of paintings)

Meyer Schapiro. *Van Gogh* (The Library of Great Painters). New York, Harry N. Abrams, 1950

ACKNOWLEDGMENTS

In a book of art, it seems particularly fitting to acknowledge the work of craftsmen who contribute to its making. The color plates were made by Litho-Art, Inc., New York. The lithography is from the presses of The Meehan-Tooker Co., Inc., New York and the binding has been done by F. M. Charlton Co., New York. The paper was made by P. H. Glatfelter Co., Spring Grove, Pa. Our deepest indebtedness is to the museums, galleries, and private collectors who graciously permitted the reproduction of their paintings, drawings, and sculpture.